Al-Ghazzali On Knowing This World and the Hereafter

Ḥujjat al-Islām Abū Ḥāmid
Muḥammad Ghazzālī Ṭūsī

Translated from the Persian by
Muhammad Nur Abdus Salam

Introduction by
Laleh Bakhtiar

Series Editor
Seyyed Hossein Nasr

Great Books of the Islamic World

Library of Congress Cataloging-in-Publication Data

Ḥujjat al-Islām Abū Ḥāmid Muḥammad Ghazzālī Ṭūsī (AH450/CE1059 to AH505/CE1111), commonly known as al-Ghazzali. *On Knowing This World and the Hereafter* from the *Alchemy of Happiness (Kimiya al-saadat),* the Persian translation by al-Ghazzali of the *Ihya ulum al-din (Revival of the Religious Sciences)*

1. Islamic psychology. 2. Sufism. 3. Islamic theology—Early works to 1800. 4. Ghazzali, 1058-1111. I. Title.

ISBN: 1-57644-682-5 pbk

Cover design: Liaquat Ali

Cornerstones are Allah and Muhammad connected by *Bismillāh al-Raḥmān al-Raḥīm* (In the Name of God, the Merciful, the Compassionate).

Logo design by Mani Ardalan Farhadi

The cypress tree bending with the wind, the source for the paisley design, is a symbol of the perfect Muslim, who, as the tree, bends with the wind of God's Will.

Published by
Great Books of the Islamic World, Inc.
Distributed by
KAZI Publications, Inc.
3023 W. Belmont Avenue
Chicago IL 60618
Tel: 773-267-7001; FAX: 773-267-7002
email: info@kazi.org /www.kazi.org

Introduction

". . . be not like those who forgot God and [eventually] God caused them to forget their 'self' . . . " (Q. 59:18-19)

There is nothing more timely today than a translation of the remarkable work on Islam of al-Ghazzali for two reasons. First of all, the results of recent studies of medicine psychology and religious belief[1] confirm that the religious model works in the healing process so traditional wisdom must be made available in English for all researchers as well as readers to be able to access it and draw upon it for areas of further research. Secondly, at a time when the world is confused by the varying beliefs of Muslims and are interested in studying what the majority of the world's Muslims believe, the works of al-Ghazzali provide the perfect opportunity.

Abu Hamid Muhammad al-Ghazzali was born in the city of Tus, northwestern Iran, in AD 1058.[2] He studied in Tus until he was twenty-seven when he moved to Baghdad. He was appointed as a professor at the Nizamiyyah college there when he was thirty-three. After four years of a strenuous schedule, he underwent a spiritual experience which convinced him that all of the knowledge he had gained was useless in comparison to gnosis or experiential knowledge of the Divine Presence. He realized unless he left his position and was free to search for this knowledge deeper within himself without worldly distractions, he would never attain it. He therefore provided for his family and left for Damascus and other well known cities at that time.

When he was forty-eight he returned to his birthplace where he lived for the next five years until his early death at the age of fifty-three.[3] He left behind over 400 works among them being his famous *Revival of the Religious Sciences* (*Ihya ulum al-din*) which he wrote in Arabic. Over 2300 pages, it is a compendium of Islamic practices. A few years after he finished the *Revival*, he felt the need to write the same sort of compendium on being a Muslim in Persian. This is the entire work here translated into English for the first time which al-Ghazzali called the *Alchemy of Happiness*. It is a masterful textbook on traditional psychology.[4]

Notes to the Introduction

1 See works like *Timeless Healing: The Power and Biology of Belief* by Herbert Benson; *Why God Won't Go Away: Brain Science and the Biology of Belief* by Andrew Newberg, Eugene D'Aquili and Vince Rause; and *Handbook of Religion and Health* edited by Harold G. Koniz, Michael McCullough and David B. Larsen.

2 Other well known writers and poets born in Tus include Abu Yazid Bistami, Husayn bin Mansur Hallaj, Abu Said Abi'l-Khayr, Nizam al-Mulk, Firdawsi and Umar Khayyam.

3 See the following Bibliography for the numerous books that detail the life of al-Ghazzali. It is interesting to note that al-Ghazzali wrote the *Alchemy of Happiness* when the First Crusade ruled Jerusalem. Saladin arrived on the scene seventy-seven years after al-Ghazzali's death.

4 Traditional psychology historically was called the science of ethics or practical wisdom (*hikmat al-amali*).

Bibliography

al-Ghazzali. *Alchemy of Happiness* abridged. Translated by Claud Field. Lahore: Sh. Muhammad Ashraf, 1987. 1100 pages summarized in 60 pages.

al-Ghazzali. *Alchemy of Happiness*. Complete translation by Jay R. Crook. Chicago: Kazi Publications, 2002.

al-Ghazzali. *Confessions*. Translated by Claud Field. Lahore: Sh. Muhammad Ashraf, 1992.

al-Ghazzali. *Deliverance from Error*. Translated by R. J. McCarthy. KY: fons vitae, 1980.

al-Ghazzali. *Faith in Divine Unity and Trust in Divine Providence*. Translated from the *Ihya ulum al-din* (*Kitab al-tawhid wa'l tawakkul*). Translated by David B. Burrell. Cambridge: Islamic Texts Society, 2001.

al-Ghazzali. *Ihya ulum al-din* (*Revival of the Religious Sciences*). Translated by al-Hajj Maulana Fazul ul-Karim. Lahore: Islamic Publications Bureau, n.d.

al-Ghazzali, *Incoherence of the Philosophers*. Translated by Michael E. Marmura. A parallel English-Arabic text. Provo, Utah: Brigham University Press, 1952.

al-Ghazzali. *Inner Dimensions of Islamic Worship*. Translated from the *Ihya ulum al-din*. Leicester; Islamic Foundation, 1990.

al-Ghazzali. *Invocations and Supplications*. Translated from the *Ihya ulum al-din* (*Kitab al-adhkar wal daawat*) by K. Nakamura. Cambridge: Islamic Texts Society, 1996.

al-Ghazzali, *Just Balance* (*al-Qistas al-mustaqim*), Translated by D. P. Brewster. Lahore, Pakistan: Sh. Muhammad Ashraf, 1987.

al-Ghazzali. *Letters of al-Ghazzali*. Translated by Abdul Qayyum. Lahore: Islamic Publications (Pvt), Ltd. , 1994.

al-Ghazzali. *Mishkat al-anwar*. Translated by W. H. T. Gairdner. Lahore: Sh. Muhammad Ashraf, 1991.

al-Ghazzali. *Mysteries of Almsgiving*. Translated from the *Ihya ulum al-din* (*Kitab asrar al-zakah*) by Nabih Amin Faris. Lahore: Sh. Muhammad Ashraf, 1992.

al-Ghazzali, *Mysteries of Fasting*. Translated from the *Ihya ulum al-din* by Nabih Amin Faris. Lahore: Sh. Muhammad Ashraf, 1992.

al-Ghazzali. *Mysteries of Purity*. Translated from the *Ihya ulum al-din* by Nabih Amir Faris. Lahore: Sh. Muhammad Ashraf, 1991.

al-Ghazzali. *Mysteries of Worship*. Translated from the *Ihya ulum al-din* by Edwin Elliot Calverley. Lahore: Sh. Muhammad Ashraf, 1998.

al-Ghazzali, *Niche of Lights*. Translated by David Buchman. A parallel English-Arabic text. Provo, Utah: Brigham university Press, 1998.

al-Ghazzali. *Ninety-nine Beautiful Names of God* (*al-Maqsad al-asna fi sharh asma Allah al-husna*). Translated by David B. Burrell and Nazih Daher. Cambridge: Islamic Texts Society, 1999.

Al-Ghazzali On Disciplining the Self. Translated from the *Alchemy of Happiness* by Muhammad Nur Abdus Salam (Jay R. Crook). Chicago: Kazi Publications, 2002.

al-Ghazzali. *On Disciplining the Soul and the Two Desires*. Translated from the *Ihya ulum al-din* (*Kitab riyadat al-nafs. Kitab kasr al-shahwatayn)* by T. J. Winter. Cambridge: Islamic Texts Society, 2001.

al-Ghazzali. *On Divine Predicates and their Properties* (*al-Iqtisad fil'itiqad*). Translated by Abdu Rahman Abu Zayd. India: Kitab Bhavan, 1994.

Al-Ghazzali On Earning a Living and Trade. Translated from *Alchemy of Happiness* by Muhammad Nur Abdus Salam (Jay R. Crook). Chicago: Kazi Publications, 2002.

Al-Ghazzali On Enjoining Good and Forbidding Wrong. Translated from *Alchemy of Happiness* by Muhammad

Nur Abdus Salam (Jay R. Crook). Chicago: Kazi Publications, 2002.

Al-Ghazzali On Governing and Managing the State. Translated from *Alchemy of Happiness* by Muhammad Nur Abdus Salam (Jay R. Crook). Chicago: Kazi Publications, 2002.

Al-Ghazzali On Hope and Fear. Translated from *Alchemy of Happiness* by Muhammad Nur Abdus Salam (Jay R. Crook). Chicago: Kazi Publications, 2002.

Al-Ghazzali On Journeying. Translated from *Alchemy of Happiness* by Muhammad Nur Abdus Salam (Jay R. Crook). Chicago: Kazi Publications, 2002.

Al-Ghazzali On Knowing This World and the Hereafter. Translated from *Alchemy of Happiness* by Muhammad Nur Abdus Salam (Jay R. Crook). Chicago: Kazi Publications, 2002.

Al-Ghazzali On Knowing Yourself and God. Translated from *Alchemy of Happiness* by Muhammad Nur Abdus Salam (Jay R. Crook). Chicago: Kazi Publications, 2002.

Al-Ghazzali On Listening to Music. Translated from *Alchemy of Happiness* by Muhammad Nur Abdus Salam (Jay R. Crook). Chicago: Kazi Publications, 2002.

Al-Ghazzali On Love, Longing and Contentment. Translated from *Alchemy of Happiness* by Muhammad Nur Abdus Salam (Jay R. Crook). Chicago: Kazi Publications, 2002.

Al-Ghazzali On Marriage. Translated from *Alchemy of Happiness* by Muhammad Nur Abdus Salam (Jay R. Crook). Chicago: Kazi Publications, 2002.

Al-Ghazzali On Meditation. Translated from *Alchemy of Happiness* by Muhammad Nur Abdus Salam (Jay R. Crook). Chicago: Kazi Publications, 2002.

Al-Ghazzali On Patience and Gratitude. Translated from *Alchemy of Happiness* by Muhammad Nur Abdus Salam (Jay R. Crook). Chicago: Kazi Publications, 2002.

Al-Ghazzali On Reckoning and Guarding. Translated from *Alchemy of Happiness* by Muhammad Nur Abdus Salam (Jay R. Crook). Chicago: Kazi Publications, 2002.

Al-Ghazzali On Remembering Death and the States of the Hereafter. Translated from *Alchemy of Happiness* by Muhammad Nur Abdus Salam (Jay R. Crook). Chicago: Kazi Publications, 2002.

Al-Ghazzali On Repentance. Translated from *Alchemy of Happiness* by Muhammad Nur Abdus Salam (Jay R. Crook). Chicago: Kazi Publications, 2002.

Al-Ghazzali On Spiritual Poverty and Asceticism. Translated from *Alchemy of Happiness* by Muhammad Nur Abdus Salam (Jay R. Crook). Chicago: Kazi Publications, 2002.

Al-Ghazzali On Sufism. Translated from *Alchemy of Happiness* by Muhammad Nur Abdus Salam (Jay R. Crook). Chicago: Kazi Publications, 2002.

Al-Ghazzali On the Duties of Brotherhood. Translated from *Alchemy of Happiness* by Muhammad Nur Abdus Salam (Jay R. Crook). Chicago: Kazi Publications, 2002.

Al-Ghazzali On the Etiquette of Eating. Translated from *Alchemy of Happiness* by Muhammad Nur Abdus Salam (Jay R. Crook). Chicago: Kazi Publications, 2002.

al-Ghazzali. *On the Foundations of the Articles of Faith*. Translated from the *Ihya ulum al-din* (*Kitab qawaid al-aqaid*) by Nabih Amir Faris. Lahore: Sh. Muhammad Ashraf, 1999.

Al-Ghazzali On the Lawful, the Unlawful and the Doubtful. Translated from *Alchemy of Happiness* by Muhammad Nur Abdus Salam (Jay R. Crook). Chicago: Kazi Publications, 2002.

al-Ghazzali. *On the Manners Relating to Eating*. Translated from the *Ihya ulum al-din* (*Kitab adab al-akl*) by D. Johnson-Davies. Cambridge: Islamic Texts Society, 2000.

Al-Ghazzali On the Mysteries of the Pillars of Islam.

Translated from *Alchemy of Happiness* by Muhammad Nur Abdus Salam (Jay R. Crook). Chicago: Kazi Publications, 2002.

Al-Ghazzali On the Treatment of Anger, Hatred and Envy. Translated from *Alchemy of Happiness* by Muhammad Nur Abdus Salam (Jay R. Crook). Chicago: Kazi Publications, 2002.

Al-Ghazzali On the Treatment of Hypocrisy. Translated from *Alchemy of Happiness* by Muhammad Nur Abdus Salam (Jay R. Crook). Chicago: Kazi Publications, 2002.

Al-Ghazzali On the Treatment of Ignorance Arising from Heedlessness, Error and Delusion. Translated from *Alchemy of Happiness* by Muhammad Nur Abdus Salam (Jay R. Crook). Chicago: Kazi Publications, 2002.

Al-Ghazzali On the Treatment of Love for This World. Translated from *Alchemy of Happiness* by Muhammad Nur Abdus Salam (Jay R. Crook). Chicago: Kazi Publications, 2002.

Al-Ghazzali On the Treatment of Love of Power and Control. Translated from *Alchemy of Happiness* by Muhammad Nur Abdus Salam (Jay R. Crook). Chicago: Kazi Publications, 2002.

Al-Ghazzali On the Treatment of Miserliness and Greed. Translated from *Alchemy of Happiness* by Muhammad Nur Abdus Salam (Jay R. Crook). Chicago: Kazi Publications, 2002.

Al-Ghazzali On the Treatment of Pride and Conceit. Translated from *Alchemy of Happiness* by Muhammad Nur Abdus Salam (Jay R. Crook). Chicago: Kazi Publications, 2002.

Al-Ghazzali On the Treatment of the Harms of the Tongue. Translated from *Alchemy of Happiness* by Muhammad Nur Abdus Salam (Jay R. Crook). Chicago: Kazi Publications, 2002.

Al-Ghazzali On the Treatment of the Lust of the Stomach and the Sexual Organs. Translated from *Alchemy of Happiness* by Muhammad Nur Abdus Salam (Jay R. Crook). Chicago: Kazi Publications, 2002.

Al-Ghazzali On Trust and the Unity of God. Translated from *Alchemy of Happiness* by Muhammad Nur Abdus Salam (Jay R. Crook). Chicago: Kazi Publications, 2002.

Al-Ghazzali On Truthfulness and Sincerity. Translated from *Alchemy of Happiness* by Muhammad Nur Abdus Salam (Jay R. Crook). Chicago: Kazi Publications, 2002.

al-Ghazzali. *Path to Sufism*. Translated by R. J. McCarthy. KY: fons vitae, 2001.

al-Ghazzali. *Some Moral and Religious Teachings*. Translated by Syed Nawab Ali. Lahore: Sh. Muhammad Ashraf, 1995.

al-Ghazzali. *Remembrance of Death and the Afterlife*. Translated from the *Ihya ulum al-din* (*Kitab dhikr al-mawt wa-ma-badahun*) by T. J. Winter. Cambridge: Islamic Texts Society, 1999.

al-Ghazzali. *The Duties of Brotherhood*. Translated from the *Ihya ulum al-din*. Leicester: Islamic Foundation, 1990.

al-Ghazzali. *The Mystic*. Margaret Smith. Chicago: Kazi Publications, 2002.

Avicenna. *The Canon of Medicine*. Chicago: Kazi Publications, 1999.

Benson, Herbert. *Timeless Healing: The Power and Biology of Belief*. NY: Simon and Schuster, 1996.

Ethical Philosophy of al-Ghazzali. Muhammad Umar ud-Din. Lahore: Sh. Muhammad Ashraf, 1991.

Faith and Practice of al-Ghazzali. W. Montgomery Watt. Edinburgh: Edinburgh University Press, 1952. An abridged translation of *Munqidh min ad-dalal* (Deliverance from Error) and the Beginning of Guidance (*Bidayat al-hidayah*).

Fakhry, Majid. *Al-Ghazzali's Theory of Virtue*. NY: SUNY,

1985.
Koniz, Harold G., Michael McCullough and David B. Larsen. *Handbook of Religion and Health*. NY: Oxford University Press, 2001.
Newberg, Andrew, Eugene D'Aquili and Vince Rause. *Why God Won't Go Away: Brain Science and the Biology of Belief*. NY: Ballantine Books, 2002.

Al-Ghazzali On Knowing This World

1 The Reason for Us Being in the World

Know that the world is a stage of the stages on the way of religion, a passing place for the travelers to the Divine Presence, a decked-out market placed at the edge of the desert from which the travelers take provisions.

This world and the Hereafter comprise two states: that which is prior to death and nearer to you and which is called the world; and that which is after death, called the Hereafter. The purpose of the world is the provisioning for the Hereafter. A human being is created plain and lacking at the beginning of his creation, but has the potential to achieve perfection and to make the celestial image the design of his heart so as to be fitting for the Divine Presence in the sense that he finds a way to become one of the beholders of the beauty of the Presence. This is the farthest limit of his (spiritual) happiness. This is his Paradise. This is why he was created!

But he cannot become a beholder so long as his eyes are not opened, nor can he perceive that Beauty. That comes with gnosis (*marifat*). The key to the knowledge of the Divine Beauty is knowledge of the wonders of the Divine handiwork. And the (five) human sensory organs are the first key to the Divine handiwork. These senses would not have been possible except in this body compounded of water and earth.

So, this is the reason he has fallen into the world of water and earth, so that he may gather his provisions and obtain the gnosis (*marifat*) of God Most High with the key of the knowledge of his own self and the knowledge of all quarters of the world perceptible to the senses. As long as a person possesses these senses and they spy out things for him, he is said to be "in the world." When he says farewell to these senses, while he endures as do those things which are the essence of his attributes, then it is said that "he has gone to the Hereafter." As a consequence, this is the reason for his being in the world.

2 The True Nature, Bane, and Purpose of the World

So, a person needs two things in the world: one is to obtain nourishment for his heart to protect if from the causes of destruction; and the other is to obtain nourishment for his body to protect it from the Destroyers. The nourishment of the heart is the gnosis and love of God Most High. The nourishment of every thing is according to its nature, for that is its natural disposition. It has previously been made clear that this is the natural disposition of a human being. The reason for the destruction of a human being is his becoming absorbed in something other than God Most High.

The body must be tended by the spirit, for the body is mortal while the spirit is immortal. The body for the spirit is like a camel for the pilgrim on the road to perform the pilgrimage; the camel is for the pilgrim, not the pilgrim for the camel, even though the pilgrim is necessarily obligated to provide it with fodder, water, and covering until he reaches the Kabah and is relieved of this trouble. However, his obligation must be according to need. If he spends all of this time in feeding, adorning, and tending (the camel), the caravan will leave him behind and he will perish. In the same manner, if a person spends all of his time tending his body so that he will increase his strength and keep dangerous things away, he will be deprived of his own (spiritual) happiness.

The body needs three things in the world: food, clothing, and shelter. Food is for nourishment, clothing and shelter are for cold and heat, to prevent them from killing him. A person's needs for his body are no more than these; indeed, these are the foundations of the world itself.

The nourishment of the heart is gnosis (*marifat*), the more the better; while the nourishment of the body is food; (but) should you eat too much of it, it may cause your death. However, it is for this that God Most High has appointed an appetite (*shahwat*) over a human being to prompt him with respect to food, clothing, and shelter, lest his body—his steed—perish. This appetite is created in such a way so that it does not limit itself, but (continually) desires more. Reason has been created to restrain it, and the Religious Law has been sent by means of the tongues of the prophets to elucidate it.

However, the carnal appetite was created first, for an infant has need of it. Reason was created afterwards. Thus, lust took its place from the beginning and became established firmly. It continuously resists reason and the Religious Law, which came to him later, so as not to permit his totality to engage in the quest for food, clothing, and shelter and for that reason forget his self and not know what this food and clothing are needed for and why he came into this world and (so as not to) forget the nourishment of the heart, which is the provision for the Hereafter. From all this, you know the true nature, bane, and purpose of the world. Now you should learn the branches and activities of the world.

3 The Bases of the World: Food, Clothing, and Shelter

Know that when you examine the details of the world, you

find that it is comprised of three things: First, the most noble of things which have been created upon the face of the earth, such as plants, metals, and animals. In reality, land is necessary for dwellings and for the use of agriculture. Metals, such as copper, bronze, and iron (are necessary) for tools; and animals for transportation and food. A human being has busied his animal soul and body with these things, be it the heart busying itself with their love and acquisition, or the body with their improvement and taking care of them.

Traits that cause its ruin, such as greed, miserliness, envy, enmity, etc., will appear in the heart as a result of its being engaged with the love for these things. And these traits in the heart arise from the entanglement of the body with (the world) to the extent that one forgets one's self, devoting all to worldly affairs.

Just as the basis of the world is three things—food, clothing, and shelter—the basis of the arts—which are a human necessity—are also three things: farming, weaving, and construction. Each one of these has branches. Some are preparatory, such as the cotton carder and the spinner who prepares (the thread) for the weaver; while others finish the work, such as the tailor who finishes what the weaver has begun. All of these require implements made of wood, iron, leather, and the like; thus, the blacksmith, carpenter, and the cobbler come into existence.

When all of these have appeared, they need to help each other, for each person cannot do all of these jobs by himself. So they come together. The tailor does work for the weaver and the blacksmith; the blacksmith takes care of the needs of the other two. In this fashion each one works for the others.

Eventually, transactions appear among them from which antagonisms arise, for each person may not be satisfied with his own portion, and they may attack each other. As a result, they find themselves in the need for three more arts: one, the art of politics and rule; two, the art of adjudication and government; and three, the art of religious jurisprudence by which the law of mediation among the people may be known. Each one of these is a trade, although most of their work is not related to the hands.

In this manner, the vocations of the world multiplied and became interrelated. The people lost themselves among them and did not know that the root of all of these was no more than three things: food, clothing, and shelter. All of this became necessary for (satisfying) those three needs, and those three are necessary for the body, and the body is necessary for the heart, to serve as its vehicle. The heart is necessary for God. But they forget themselves and they forget God, like the pilgrim who forgets himself, the Kabah, and (the object of) his journey and spends all of his time in taking care of his camel!

So the world and the real nature of the world is what has been said above. He who is not prepared and alert, does not have his eye fixed on the Hereafter, and is not occupied with the world more than necessary, has not come to know the world. The cause of this is ignorance, as the Prophet (ﷺ) said: "The world is more of a sorcerer than were Harut and Marut; beware of it!"

Since the world is so bewitching, it behooves us to know its treachery and deceit, and to enlighten the people with examples of its works. Accordingly, it is now the time for you to hear some of these examples.

4 Examples of the Sorcery of the World and the Heedlessness of Its Inhabitants

The first example: The first sorcery of the world is that it shows itself to you so that you suppose that the world is itself unmoving and is settled down firmly with you, yet it is continuously fleeing from you! However, it moves gradually, and bit by bit. It is like a shadow: when you look at it, it appears still; but it is always moving. It is obvious that your life is doing the same, always going. Gradually, moment by moment, it is growing less. That is the world which is fleeing from you and bidding you farewell; but you are unaware!

Another example: Its spell is that it feigns friendship in order to make of you its lover. Moreover, it pretends to you to have come to a living arrangement with you and will not go to another. Then, suddenly, it becomes your enemy! It is like a depraved, worthless woman who tricks men into becoming her lovers. Then she takes them home and kills them. Jesus (عليه السلام) in his own revelations, saw the world in the shape of an old woman. He asked her: "How many husbands have you had?" She replied: "Too many to count." He said: "Did they die or divorce you?" She said: "Neither; I slew them all." Jesus said: "How strange it is that those other fools who saw what you had done to the others, nevertheless desired you and did not learn the lesson."

Another example: The sorcery of the world is that its exterior is adorned attractively while everything of its calamities and sufferings is concealed, so that the ignorant will look at the appearance and be deluded. Its similitude is the veiled, ugly old crone who dresses in garments of silk brocade and wears many beautiful ornaments so that anyone who sees her from a distance will be attracted to her. But when he lifts the veil, he is filled with regret and sees her infamies.

In the Traditions it is related that the world will be summoned on the Day of Resurrection in the form of an ugly, toothless, green-eyed old hag so that the people may look at her and say: "We seek refuge with God! What is this, with this disgrace and with this ugliness?" They will reply: "This is the world for which you envied and fought each other, shed blood, and betrayed the bonds of kinship. This is what attracted you!" At the moment she is thrown into hell, she will cry: "O

Lord God! Where are my lovers?" He will command that they be thrown into hell after her.

Another example: A person who takes into account how long was the part of eternity when he did not exist in he world, and how long he will be in eternity when he is not in the world, how few these days are between pre-eternity and unending eternity, he knows that the metaphor of the world is the road of a traveler. At the beginning it is a cradle and at the end a grave. In between there are a limited number of stations. While he is traveling, every year is like a station, every month a parasang, and every day a mile, and every breath a step. For one (person) a parasang of the journey is left, for another less than a parasang, for others more or less. And that person who sits calmly, as it were, as though he would always be here, makes arrangements that he will not need for ten years in the future—in two days he will be under the earth!

Another example: Know that the similitude of the inhabitants of the world in the enjoyment of what they obtain compared with that disgrace and sorrow they will see from the world in the Hereafter is the person who gorges himself on delicious, fat, and sweet food until he ruins his stomach. Then, he perceives a stench and vileness in his bowels, his breath, and his stools. Then, he is put to shame and regrets that the pleasure is gone but the unpleasantness remains: the more delicious the food, the more fetid the stools. However much the pleasure of the world is greater, the greater will be the disgrace in the end. This itself will become evident when the spirit is torn (from the body): whoever more enjoyed the ease, orchards, gardens, serving girls and boys, gold, and silver, will, at the time of death, have more sorrow, tribulation, and torment than that person who possessed less. That sorrow and torment will not disappear at death; rather it will increase, for that love (of the world) is (has become) an attribute of the spirit, and the spirit will endure and not die.

Another example: Know that the affairs of the world which come before us seem trivial. People think that their work will not take long, but perhaps a minor thing will bring about a hundred things. Jesus (عليه السلام) says: "The seeker of the world is like one who drinks water from the sea. The more he drinks the thirstier he becomes. He drinks until he perishes, and the thirst never passes from him." Our Prophet (ﷺ) says: "Just as it is not possible for a person to enter the water without getting wet, it is not possible for a person to engage in the affairs of the world without getting tainted."

Another example: The similitude of the person who comes into the world is that of the person who becomes the guest of a host whose custom it is to always keep his hall prepared for guests. He invites them, group after group. He places a golden platter before him. On it are sugarplums and a silver censer with fragrant aloeswood and incense to perfume him and make him pleasant smelling. He eats the sugarplums and passes the tray and censer to others. Each who knows the etiquette and is intelligent in turn sniffs the aloeswood and incense and perfumes himself and eats of the sugarplums and passes the tray and censer to the next in good spirits, (then) he expresses his gratitude and departs. But the person who is a fool thinks that they were given to him and takes them with him. When they are taken back from him at the time of departure, he is unhappy and displeased, and he protests!

The world, too, is like an inn, a stopping place for travelers so that they may to gather the provisions for the rest of the journey. They should not covet anything in the inn.

Another example: The inhabitants of the world with their attachment to the affairs of the world and their forgetting the Hereafter are like some people on a ship who come to an island. They go ashore to take care of their physical needs and for purification. The captain calls out to them: "Do not delay; just purify yourselves. The ship will depart shortly."

The people spread out over the island. The more intelligent purify themselves quickly and return. They find the ship empty, so they occupy the more pleasant and more favorable places. Another group lose themselves in the marvels of the island and stand admiring the fine flowers, song birds, and colorful, patterned pebbles. When they return, they found no open places and sit crowded together in the dark, and they suffer from that.

Another group does not content themselves with merely looking. They collect some of the fine, strange, colorful stones and bring them back to the ship with them. They find no places to sit comfortably and sit pressed together. They hang the colorful stones and buttercups around their necks. After one or two days, those beautiful colors change and become dark. The odor of the flowers begins to become unpleasant. They cannot find any place to throw them down. They regret what they have done and bear their sorrow for it on their necks.

Another group falls under the spell of the island and goes off like tourists until they are so far from the ship that they do not hear the captain's summons. They are left on the island until some of them perish from hunger, and the others are killed by wild beasts.

The first group are like the abstemious believers, and the last are like the unbelievers who have forgotten God, self, and the Hereafter. All of those others have given themselves to the world: *They have chosen the life of the world over the Hereafter*. (Q. 16:107) The two groups in between are like rebels who have preserved the basis of faith, but have not abstained from the world: one group took pleasure in spiritual poverty (*darwishi*), and the other group accumulated many comforts with pleasure, until they became a heavy burden.

5 Not Everything in the World Is Blameworthy

With this previous censure of the world, do not think that everything in the world is forbidden; rather, there are things in the world that are not of the world. In what way? Knowledge and deeds are in the world, but not of it, for they accompany a person to the Hereafter. Knowledge itself will endure with him exactly (as it is); however, as for one's deeds, though they will not endure precisely as they were, their effect will remain. This is divided into two parts: one is the cleanliness and purity of the essence of the heart, which are attained by means of abandoning sin: and the other is the fondness for the remembrance of God Most High which is attained by caution in worship. So, these two are among the good deeds that endure, as God Most High said: *And the good deeds which endure are better in thy Lord's sight for reward.* (Q. 19:76)

The pleasure of knowledge, the pleasure of intimate conversation with God, and the pleasure of the fondness for remembering God Most High are better than all other pleasures. They are in the world, but not of it. Consequently, all pleasures are not blameworthy, just the pleasure which passes or does not endure. These too are not all censured, for there are two kinds: one is that which, although of the world and perishing after death, such as food, conjugal intercourse, clothing, and shelter in measure according to need, yet is a helper for the work of the Hereafter, for knowledge and deeds, and for the increase of (the number of) believers, as this is a condition of the road to the Hereafter. Every person who is satisfied with this much of the world and whose aim from it is rendering aid to religious work is not worldly.

Therefore, (those things) of the world are reprehensible the purpose of which is not to further the work of religion; indeed, they are the cause of heedlessness, *hubris*, the establishment of the animal soul in this world, and the abhorrence of the next world. It was for this that the Prophet (ﷺ) said: "The world and all that is in it is accursed save the remembrance of God Most High, and that which supports him in that."

Let this much suffice in explanation of the true nature and purpose of the world. . . .

Al-Ghazzali
On Knowing the Hereafter

1 Physical and Spiritual Heaven and Hell

Know that no one recognizes the real nature of the Hereafter until he first recognizes the true nature of death. He does not know the true nature of death until he knows the true nature of life. He does not recognize the true nature of life until he recognizes the true nature of the spirit; and the gnosis (*marifat*) of the true nature of the spirit is the gnosis of the true nature of his own self, about which something has already been explained.

Know from what has been said before, a person is compounded of two basic things: one, the heart; the other, the physical body. The heart is like the rider and the body like the mount. By means of the body this heart has a state in the Hereafter that is (either) destined for Paradise or destined for hell. By reason of its own essence it also has a state in which the body does not participate, and is destined for (either) spiritual happiness or misery. We name that ease and pleasure of the heart which is unconnected to the body "Spiritual Paradise" and we call the sorrow, pain, and misery of the heart which is unconnected to the body "Spiritual Fire."

As for the heaven and hell when the body is present, that itself is obvious. The harvest of the former is rivers, trees, the pure ones, food, drink, etc.; while the harvest of hell is fire, reptiles, scorpions, the tree of Zaqqum, etc. The descriptions in the Quran and Traditions of both of these are well-known and are comprehensible by all, while the particulars have been discussed in the book *The Remembrance of Death* (*Dhikr al-mawt*) in the *Revival*. We shall confine ourselves here to an exposition about the true nature of death and refer to the meaning of spiritual heaven and hell, something which every one does not know.

That which He said—I have prepared for My righteous worshippers that which the eye has not seen, the ear has not heard, and which has not occurred to the heart of the human being—is about spiritual heaven. From within the heart there is an opening to the spiritual world through which these sublime realities are revealed. No doubt will remain about this. The clear certainty of the happiness and the punishment of the Hereafter is made manifest to the person for whom this way is opened, not by way hearsay; rather, by way of perception and witnessing. Indeed, just as a physician recognizes whether the body is well or miserable in this world—that which is called good health or illness, for which there are reasons such as restraint and abstention (for the former) and over-eating and self-indulgence (for the latter)—in the same manner, it becomes plain with this witnessing that there is a happiness and a distress for the heart; that is, the spirit. Worship and gnosis nourish that happiness, whilst ignorance and sin is poisonous to it. That is an extremely rare knowledge.

Most of those who are called religious scholars neglect this. Indeed, they deny it! They do not go beyond the heaven and hell of the body. They know nothing about the knowledge of the Hereafter save (what has come down to them of) by report and authority. We have written many long books in Arabic in the explanation and investigation of this proof. In this book enough is said so that a quick-witted person whose mind is clear of contamination, fanaticism, and blind authority, will regain it and the affair of the Hereafter will become firm and strong in his heart; for the belief of most people in the Hereafter is weak and unstable.

2 The True Nature of Death

If you wish to know something about the true nature of death; that is, what its meaning is; know that a person has two spirits. One is of the nature of the spirit of animals, and we call it the "animal spirit." The other is of the kind of the spirit of the angels and we call that the "human spirit." The heart is the source of the animal spirit—that lump of flesh placed to the left (in your chest). It is as tenuous as a vapor from the humors within the animal. An even temperament comes from that. From the heart it reaches the brain and all parts of the body by means of the arteries which have pulse and movement. This spirit is the bearer of the powers of sensory perception and motion. When it reach the brain its heat decreases and it becomes mild. The eye receives its power of sight from it, the ear receives its power of hearing from it, and so on with the other senses.

The similitude (of the animal spirit) is a lamp that moves about a house. Wherever its goes, the walls of the house become illuminated by it. So, as the illumination from the lamp appears on the walls, in the same manner the power of sight, hearing, and the other senses of this spirit in the external organs by the power of God, may He be praised and exalted, become manifest. Should an obstruction or blockage occur in any of these arteries, those organs further down remain inactive and paralyzed. There is no longer any power of perception or movement in them. A physician endeavors to open such blockages.

This spirit is like the flame of the lamp. The heart is like the wick. Food is like the oil—should the oil be exhausted, the lamp dies; and if no nourishment is received, the balanced temperament of this spirit deteriorates and the animal dies. In the same way, if there is oil, but the wick draws up too much of it, it is consumed and no longer draws the oil. In this way, after a long period of time the heart no longer accepts food. And in the same way, if something strikes the lamp, it will go out, even though the oil and wick are in place. So too, if an animal suffers a great injury, it will die.

This spirit, as long as its humors are in balance—a necessary prerequisite—receives delicate images, such as the powers of sensory perception and movement, from the lights of the heavenly angels by the command of God Most High. Should the balance of the humors deteriorate, by an excess of heat, cold, or for some other reason, it will not be fit to receive those impressions: like a mirror the surface will reflect images so long as its surface is suitable. If it becomes scratched or tarnished, it will not reflect; not because the images have been obliterated or are absent, but because its fitness to reflect them has been nullified.

In this way, the suitability of this vapor which we have designated the animal spirit is tied to the balance of the humors. If that is nullified, it will not admit of balancing. When it does not accept the powers of perceptions and motion, the limbs are deprived of its effect and fall insensate and motionless. It is said: "It died."

This is the meaning of the death of the animal spirit. The arranger of these causes—to disturb the balance of the humors—is a created being, one of those beings created by God Most High. He is called the Angel of Death. People know his name, but coming to know his true nature is lengthy.

This is the meaning of the death of animals, but the death of a human being is of a different kind, for he has the spirit which the animals have and another spirit, which we have designated the "human spirit," or "heart" in some of the previous chapters. It is not of the same kind as the other spirit, which is physical, like attenuated air or like a refined, ripened, purified mist.

But this human spirit has no body, for it does not admit of division. The knowledge of God Most High alights in it. As God Most High is Indivisible and One, the place of the One's gnosis is also one and indivisible. It does not alight in any place capable of division; rather it alights in something one and indivisible.

So, consider the wick and the flame of the lamp and the light of the lamp, all three. The wick is like the heart, the flame of the lamp is like the animal spirit, and the light of the lamp is like the human spirit. Just as the light of the lamp is insubstantial and finer than the lamp, and, you would say, cannot (itself) be observed, the human spirit is also insubstantial—an addition to the animal spirit, and is, you would say, not observable.

This is an apt comparison when you take into consideration its insubstantiality. But from another point of view it is not apt, for the light of the lamp is dependent upon the lamp and is an offshoot of it. When the lamp is rendered useless, the light perishes. However, the human spirit is not dependent upon the animal spirit; rather, it is the foundation of the animal spirit. When the animal spirit perishes, (the human spirit) does not perish. If you desire its similitude, imagine a light which is more delicate than that lamp and (imagine) that the existence of the lamp is dependent upon (the light), not the light upon the lamp. Then the comparison will be apt.

Therefore, in one way the animal spirit is like a vehicle for the human spirit; and in another, a tool. When the constitution of this animal spirit is destroyed, the form perishes, but the human spirit remains in place, however without a tool and a vehicle. The death of the vehicle and the spoiling of the tool does not mean the harm and annihilation of the rider; but he is (left) without implements.

The implement given him was given so that he might hunt gnosis and the love of God Most High. If he has taken the prey, the loss of his implements is a blessing, removing a burden from him. This is what the Prophet (ﷺ) said: "Death is a gift and a present for the believer." It is as though a person has a net for trapping and always lugs it about. When he has captured his prey, the loss of the net is a windfall for him. If, God forbid, this tool is made useless before capturing the prey, his regret and trouble will have no end. This pain and regret is the beginning of the torment of the grave, may God save us from that!

3 Your You-ness Is Not in Your Body

Now, know that if a person's arms and legs are paralyzed, he may survive, for his true nature is not in them. Arms and legs are his tools and he employs them. Just as the true nature of your "you-ness" is not in your arms and legs, so it is not in your back, stomach, or head; nor anywhere (else) in your physical body. If all should become paralyzed, it is possible that one may survive. The meaning of death is that all parts of the body become paralyzed, but the meaning of paralysis of the hand is that it does not act at your command. Why? Because the obedience (to you) which it possessed was by way of an attribute called "power." That attribute is a light which comes to it from the lamp of the animal spirit. Should the arteries, which are the pathways of that spirit, become blocked, the power departs (from the hand) and obedience became impossible. In the same manner, the obedience which all parts of the body have to you is by virtue of the animal spirit. So, when its temperament is destroyed and obedience ceases, it is called "death." But you survive, even though your being obeyed (by the body and its parts) does not survive.

How can the true nature of your you-ness be in this body? If you think about it, you will realize that these parts of you are not the same parts as those you possessed when a child. They have all dissolved and been replaced by others with the food (you have consumed). The body is not the same (that you had then), but you are the same you! Therefore, your you-ness does not lie in your body. If your body is destroyed, so be it! You continue to live in your essential self.

However, your attributes are of two kinds: one kind is shared with your body, such as hunger, thirst, and sleep. They cannot be satisfied without stomach and body. They are canceled at the time of death. The other is that in which the body has no part, such as the knowledge of God Most High and beauty of the Divine Presence, and the joy that comes with that. This attribute is of your essence and endures with you. This is the meaning of: *Enduring good deeds*. (Q. 18:46; 19:76) Anything other than this is ignorance of God Most High, which (ignorance) is also an attribute of your essence. This is a blindness of the spirit and the seed of *Whoso will not see here will not see in the Hereafter, and yet further from the road*. (Q. 17:72)

You will in no manner know the true nature of death until you come to recognize these two spirits, the difference between them, and their relationship to each other.

4 Preserving the Balance of the Spirit

Know, now, that this animal spirit is of this lower world and is a compound of the tenuousness of the vapor of the humors. There are four humors: blood, phlegm, yellow bile, and black bile. These four originate in water, fire, earth, and air. The discord and equilibrium of temperament comes from the differences in and degrees of heat, cold, moisture, and dryness. The object of the craft of medicine is to maintain the equilibrium of these four humors in the (animal) spirit to the end that it be fit to function as the vehicle and tool of the other spirit, that which we have called the "human spirit." That (spirit) is not of this world; rather, it is of the higher world and is of the essence of the angels. Its descent into this world is foreign to the nature of its essence; however, its exile (to this world) is to enable it to gather its provisions from guidance, as God Most High said: *We said: Go down, all of you, from hence; but verily there comes unto you from Me a guidance; and whoso follows My guidance, no fear shall come upon them, neither shall they grieve.* (Q. 2:38) And this which God Most High said: *I am about to create a mortal out of the clay, and when I have fashioned him, and breathed into him of My spirit. . .* (Q. 38:71-72) is a reference to the difference between the two spirits. He delivered one with the clay and He explained the equilibrium of this temperament when He said: "I have fashioned him," (meaning) "I have made and equipped him"—and this is the equilibrium. Then He said: "I have breathed into him of My spirit," He added this to him. The similitude of this is that of a person preparing a canvas rag so that it will catch fire. Then he takes it near the fire and blows on it until it catches fire.

Just as that lower animal spirit retains its equilibrium, and a physician comes to know the causes of that equilibrium in order to repel illness and to keep it from destruction, so there is an equilibrium for the higher human spirit—that which is the true nature of the heart which ethics and spiritual self-discipline—which are known from the Religious Law—preserve in the practice of which lies its health.

Thus, it has been made known that so long as a person does not know the true nature of a person's spirit, it is impossible that he come to know the Hereafter through insight; just as one cannot know God, may He be glorified and exalted, until he knows himself. Therefore, self-knowledge is the key to the knowledge of God and the key to knowledge of the Hereafter. The root of religion is belief in God and the Last Day. It is for this reason that we have presented this gnosis (*marifat*).

However, we have not disclosed one mystery of the mysteries of His basic qualities, for it is not permitted to utter that. Hearts could not endure it. All of the gnosis of God, may He be glorified and exalted, and of the gnosis of the Hereafter is based upon it. Try to learn it from yourself by way of earnest striving and seeking; for if you heard it from someone else, you would not have the strength to listen to it. Many have heard this attribute of God Most High and have not believed, did not have the strength to hear it, or denied it, saying: "This itself is not possible! It is not absolute incomparability; rather, it is the denial of Attributes!" So, how would you have the strength to hear it with respect to a human being?

Indeed, this Attribute with respect to God Most High is not itself found explicitly in the Quran, nor in the Traditions; also because if people should hear it, they would deny it. The prophets were advised: "Have discourse with the people according to the (levels of) their intellects." "Speak to the people what they are able to bear." It was revealed to some of the prophets: "Do not say to the people that which they do not understand, for then they will deny it and that will cause them harm."

5 The Meaning of the Gathering, Resurrection, Sending, and Return

From all of this you have learned that the true nature of the human spirit is established in its own insubstantial essence, and within the establishment of its own essence and special attributes, it has no need of physical form. Death does not mean the annihilation of that; rather, it means the end of its dominion over the physical body. The meaning of the Gathering, the Resurrection, the Sending, and the Return is not that the spirit is brought into existence again after annihilation. Rather, it means that it is given a form; that is, a form which is prepared to receive its occupation again, just as was done in the beginning. This time it is easier, because at the first time, both the spirit and the body had to be created. This time the spirit endures—that is, the human spirit—and parts of the body also endure. Their collection is easier than their invention, from our point of view and from the point of view of truth. Human qualities have no access to the Divine Intelligence, for where there is no difficulty; there is also no easiness.

The prerequisite of the Return is not that (the spirit) be given to the body which it (formerly) occupied, which was in the form of a vehicle. If the horse is changed, the rider is still the same. It has been subject to change from infancy to old age, its parts for other parts of nourishment, while it remains the same.

Therefore, the people who have stipulated this so that problems have arisen for them, to which they have given weak answers, have been delivered from that trouble, as when they have been asked: "Some people eat people; the limbs of one become the limbs of the other. To which one will the parts be given? Or, if a limb (or organ) is lost to a person and after that he performs acts of service thereby acquiring religious merit, is the severed limb returned to him (in the afterlife) or not? If it is not, how can he remain sightless, handless, or footless in heaven? How can those organs which did not participate in his deeds in this world be rewarded?"

They say idle things like this and demand answers. There is no need of such things when you have learned the true nature of the Return, which is that there is no need for the same (earthly) body. This difficulty arises because they supposed that your you-ness and your true nature are your body. As that very same body does not survive, you are not that (body)! They fall into difficulty because the premise is wrong.

6 Witnessing Heaven and Hell in This World

Certainly you may say that among the religious scholars and theologians there is the famous doctrine that the vital principle (*jan*) is obliterated at death, then comes into existence again for him, and this contradicts that (which you have said).

Know that anyone who follows the words of others is blind. This person says that he is neither of the imitators (of authority), nor of the discerning, for if he were of the discerning, he would know that the death of the body does eliminate a person's true nature; and if he were of the imitators, he would know from the Quran and the Traditions that the human spirit survives after death, and that after death, the spirits are in two categories: the wretched and the happy.

As for the happy spirits, the Glorious Quran says: *And think not of those who are killed in the way of God as dead. Nay, they are alive being provided sustenance from their Lord, rejoicing in what God has given them out of His grace.* (Q. 3:169-70)

And as for the wretched spirits, when the Prophet (ﷺ) and the Companions killed the unbelievers at (the battle of) Badr, he addressed them and called to them one by one—and they were slain-saying: "You and you! The promises that I had received from God concerning the victory over His enemies were all true and God Most High has fulfilled them. Were the promises that He gave you about the punishment after death kept or not?" The crowd who were accompanying the Prophet said: "O Prophet of God, they are a heap of corpses. Why are you speaking to them?" He answered: "By that God who commands the spirit of Muhammad, they are hearing these words better than you are, but they are incapable of replying."

Anyone who searches through the Traditions which are about the dead and their awareness of their mourners and visitors (at their graves), and that which takes place in this world, knows with certainty that their annihilation has no report in Religious Law; rather, it is reported that their mode and place have been transformed. The grave is either a cave of the caves of hell or a garden of the gardens of Paradise.

So, truly know that death never nullifies anything of your essential nature, nor of your characteristic attributes. However, your sensory organs, movements, and fancies—those which are tied to the brain and organs—cease, but you endure, alone and absolute, just as you left this place. With the death of the horse, the rider does not become a learned jurisprudent if he was a weaver; if he was blind, he does not become sighted, or if he was sighed, he does not become blind: instead, he becomes a pedestrian! The body is a vehicle, like the horse. The rider is you!

It is for this reason that for persons who become absent from their sensory perceptions, and delve into their selves, becoming engaged and immersed in the remembrance of God Most High, as is the beginning of the way of Sufism, there are the states of the Hereafter by way of the "tasting," of witnessing. Their animal spirit, even though it has not lost the equilibrium of its temperament, but appears to be afflicted or exhausted so that it does not distract a person from the true nature of his essence thereby engaging him with the self. Then his state approaches that of the state of the dead. Therefore, that which for others is disclosed at death is disclosed to him here. When he comes to himself and returns to the world of perceptions, he cannot remember most of what he experienced, but there is an effect which stays with him. If the true nature of heaven has been shown to him, its spirit, ease, joy, and delight are with him.

But if he has been shown hell, then its fatigue and lassitude are with him. If he retains something of that (experience) in his memory, he relates it. If the storehouse of the thought has made a copy of that thing—a similitude that would better remain in his memory—then he relates that, as when the Prophet (ﷺ) while performing a obligatory prayer raised his hand and announced: "A bunch of grapes from heaven has been shown to me. I wished that I could have brought them to this world." Do not suppose in reality that a bunch of imitated grapes can be brought into this world. That is impossible; if it were not, (the Prophet) would have brought them. Yet it was disclosed to him by way of witnessing. The true nature of its transformation is a lengthy lesson, and there is no need for you to pursue it.

The difference in the stations of the religious scholars is that one is all taken up to know what the bunch of heavenly grapes was, why he saw it, and the others did not! Another got no more than this, that (the Prophet) had moved his hand; therefore a minor action does not nullify formal prayer and he gives long opinions about the details of this. He thinks the beginning and end of knowledge itself is in these things, and that anyone who has learned this and is not content with that and busies himself with some other (aspect) is himself idle and is turning away from the study of Religious Law!

The point is that you not think that the Prophet (ﷺ) related a story that he had heard from Gabriel, as you comprehend the meaning of "hearing" from Gabriel—that that you have learned that meaning itself like other things, too—but that the Prophet (ﷺ) saw heaven! Yet, in reality, heaven cannot be seen in this world; instead, he went to that world and was absent from this world. This was one kind of his ascensions.

However, being absent is of two kinds: one is with the death of the animal spirit; the other with affliction of the animal spirit.

However, heaven cannot be seen in this world, just as the seven heavens and the seven climes cannot be contained in a pistachio shell. One particle of heaven could not be contained in this world; rather, as the sense of hearing is excluded from displaying the image of the heavens and earth in it as the eyes do, all of the senses of this world are excluded from all the pleasures of heaven. The senses of that world are themselves something else.

7 The Meaning of the Torment of the Grave

Now the time has come for you to learn the meaning of the torment of the grave and to know that the torment of the grave is of two kinds: spiritual and physical.

As for the physical, everyone knows this himself; but not the spiritual, except for him who has come to know himself and the true nature of his own spirit. It is established by its own essence, and does not require a body in its existence. It endures after death, for death does not obliterate it. However, death takes back his eyes, ears, and all of his sensory organs, from him. When the senses are gone; wife, offspring, wealth, property, domicile, captives, livestock, relatives, connections, and, indeed, the earth and all that is in it perceptible to the senses are taken from him. If he loved all of these things and he had surrendered his entire self to them, he would necessarily remain in the torment of his separation from them. If he was free of everything and had no beloved here (on earth), but instead was yearning for death, he will be at peace. If he had attained the love of God Most High, had become fond of remembering Him, had given all of himself to Him, and had held the chattels of this world to be irksome and a distraction, then when he dies he will reach his Beloved. Trouble and confusion will depart and he will achieve (spiritual) happiness.

Now, reflect! Is it possible for a person to know himself and recognize that he will survive (after death), and to know that all of his essential desires and cherished things are in this world, and then to wonder whether, after leaving this world, he would be in misery and torment because of his separation from his own cherished possessions? As the Prophet (ﷺ) said: Cherish (well) what you cherish, for thou shalt surely be separated from it. Or if he knows that his beloved is all God, may He be praised and exalted, and holds the world and all that it contains in contempt, except that much which is his provision, can there be a doubt that when he leaves this world he will not be liberated from sorrow and achieve ease?

Therefore, whoever knows this will have no doubt that the torment of the grave exists, but not for the pious, rather for the worldly and those who have dedicated their entire being to the world. Through this, the significance of this Tradition is made clear: The world is the prison of the believer and the paradise of the unbeliever.

8 The True Nature and Degrees of the Torment of the Grave

In so far as you have come to know the root of the torment of the grave, the cause of which is the love of this world, know that this torment is of different kinds. For some it is more and for others less, in accordance with (their surrender to) the worldly carnal appetites of the world. As a result, the torment for the person who has not bound his heart to more than one thing in all the world is not so great as the torment of that person who has lands, chattels, servants, livestock, apparel, retinue, and all the comforts of the world, and binds his heart to all of them. Indeed, in this world, if someone brings a person the news that one of his horses has been stolen, his torment is less than if he is told that ten of his horses have been stolen. If you take all of his property, his sorrow would be greater than if had been half and less than it would have been if not only all of his property, but also his wife and children and all that he had in this world—everything—had been carried off as loot and taken out of the land leaving him alone. And this is the meaning of death!

Consequently, the punishment and ease of a person is according to the slackness or tightness of his ties to the world. The torment will be very harsh for him who is favored in every way with the things of the world and who dedicates his entire being to them, as God Most High said: *That is because they love this world's life more than the Hereafter*. (Q. 16:107) Alluding to such as he, the Prophet (ﷺ) said: "Do you know what was the import of the sending down of this verse: *Verily for him there is a straitened life and We shall raise him up blind on the Day of Resurrection*"? (Q. 20:124) They said: "God and the Prophet know better." He said: "The torment of the unbeliever in the grave is that he will be put in the power by ninety-nine dragons. Do you know what these dragons are? Ninety-nine snakes, each snake having nine heads. They bite and lick him and breathe into him until that day when he will be summoned forth."

The insightful have seen these dragons with the eye of insight, but the unseeing fools say: "We looked into the grave and didn't see anything. If there were something—and our eyes are good—we would have seen something."

This fool should know that these dragons are of the essence of the spirit of the dead person and are not external to the interior of his life-spirit so that another person could see them! Indeed, this dragon was inside him prior to death, but he ignored it and did not know it. He should know that this dragon is made up of the attributes of his animal soul, and the number of its heads which branch out from it is according to the number of the branches of his blameworthy traits of character. The root of the nature of this dragon is the love of the world; then the heads which branch out from it are in the number of bad traits of character which branch out from it, such as hatred, envy, hypocrisy, arrogance, greed, deceit, fraud, enmity, the love of rank, pomp, and wealth, etc. The root of this dragon and the multitude of its heads may be recognized with the light of insight; however, their number can be seen by the light of prophethood in accordance with the number of the bad qualities that (the light) encompasses, but we have no knowledge of the number of traits

Thus, this dragon is resident and hidden inside the vital spirit (*jan*) of the unbeliever, not only because he is ignorant of God and the Prophet; but also because he has dedicated himself to the world. As God Most High said: *That is because they love this world's life more than the Hereafter*. (Q. 16:107) He also said: *Ye squandered your good things in your life of the world and sought comfort in them*. (Q. 46:20) If it were that the dragon were external to him, as some people suppose, it would have been easier; for it would have been possible that it defer (punishment) from him in an hour, but as it—the exact copy of his attributes—is established within his spirit (*jan*), how can he escape it?

Just as a person who sells a bondmaid then finds that he is in love with her, that dragon within his spirit continually stings him. It is his love which was hidden in his heart, but he was unaware of it until now when it inflicts a wound on him. Just like this one, there were ninety-nine dragons inside him before death, but he was unaware of them until now when the wound has appeared. Just as the itself was the cause of his ease as long as he was with his beloved; that same (love) became the cause of his sorrow at the time of separation, for if there had been no love, at the time of separation there would have been no sorrow, as the love of the world and his passionate love which is the cause of ease become the causes of his torment. The love of rank stings his self like a dragon, the passionate love for wealth (bites) like a snake, the passionate love for rank (stings) like a scorpion, and know that the rest are analogous to these.

As the lover of the bondmaid, in separation, desires to throw himself into water and fire, or that a scorpion sting him so that he is relieved of the pain (of separation), so (the lover of the world) will desire that the pain of the scorpion and snake were in lieu of that which torments him in the grave. For in this world people know that the former wound the body and do so from the outside, while the latter wound inside the spirit and do so from within; but no external eye sees it.

So, in reality, each person carries the cause of his own torment with him from here, and that is inside him. It was for this that the Prophet (ﷺ) said: Rather these are your deeds being returned to you. He said: "All of this punishment is nothing more than you own (deeds) placed before you." And it is for this that God Most High said: "If you had sure knowledge, you yourselves would see hell." *Nay, would that ye knew with a sure knowledge! For ye will behold hell-fire. Aye, ye will behold it with sure vision*! (Q. 102:5-7) *And for this He said: Lo! Hell is all around the disbelievers*. (Q. 9:49) Hell surrounds them and is together with them: He did not say "will be surrounding."

9 Those Things of the Next World Which Cannot Be Seen by the Eye of This World

Surely, you may say: "It is apparent from the external sense of the Law that this dragon is seen with eye of the head, but that dragon which is inside the self is not visible (to the physical eye)."

Know that this dragon is visible, but only to the dead. The people of this world do not see it, for nothing from the other world can be seen by eye of this world. This dragon is a similitude for the dead person, so that he sees it in the way that a dragon is seen in this world—but you do not see it; just as a sleeping person often sees a snake biting him, but the person sitting beside him does not see it. That snake has reality for the sleeper and he is pained by it, but is non-existent for the conscious person. The torment of the sleeper is not diminished because the wakeful person does not see the snake.

When a sleeper sees a snake bite him in a dream, it is the injury of an enemy who will obtained victory over him and that pain is spiritual and is on the heart, but its similitude—when desired (to be) borrowed from this world—is a snake. It may be that when an enemy triumphs over him, he may say: "I have seen the explanation of (my) dream." And he may say: "Would that the snake had bitten me and that enemy had not done his will with me," because that torment in his heart would be greater than the pain of the snake (bite) which would be on the body.

So, if you should say that the snake is non-existent and that that which bites the sleeper is but a phantom of the imagination, know that this is a great error. On the contrary, the snake does exist, for it has achieved the meaning of existence and not achieved the meaning of non-existence. Whatever you perceive and see in sleep has existence for you, even though no one else can see it. And whatever you do not see is unperceived and non-existent for you, even though all creation sees it! Since the torment and the cause of the torment have been perceived by both the dead person and the sleeper, what does it matter if others do not see it?

Yet there is this, that the sleeper will soon awake and be liberated from (his torment). Therefore this (torment) is called "imaginary." However, the dead person remains enveloped in (torment), for death has no end. (The torment) remains with him permanently, as firmly as the sensory perceptions of this world.

It is not found in the Religious Law that those snakes, scorpions, and dragons which are in the grave should be visible to the physical eyes of the common folk as long as they are in the visible world. However, if a person distances himself from this world by sleeping, and the state of this dead person is revealed to him, he sees him among the snakes and scorpions. The prophets and saints also see this while awake, for what others experience in sleep, they experience while awake. The world of perception does not veil their witnessing the affairs of the other world.

So this prolixity leads to this: that some fools look into a grave and do not see anything with their external eyes, so they deny the torment of the grave. This is because they do not know the way to the affair of that (other) world.

10 For Whom Is the Torment of the Grave, and for Whom Is It Not?

Surely you will say: "If the torment of the grave is because of the connection of the spirit to this world, no one is free from that who loves his wife, children, property, and rank. Consequently, everyone will be subjected to the torment of the grave and no one will escape it."

The answer to this is: "That is not the way of it, for there are people who are fed up with the world and for them no pleasure of enjoyment or tranquillity in it remains. They wish for death, and there are many Muslims like that who are poor (*darwish*). However, those who are rich and powerful are of two kinds: there is a group who, though they love the things of this world, also love God Most High. So, if the case is that they love God Most High more (than the world), then there is no torment for them. Their parable is that of a person who has a mansion and a city which he loves, but he loves governing, rule, palace, and garden even more. If a command comes to him from the king appointing him as the governor of another city, he will not regret leaving his own homeland at all, for his love for his mansion, home, and city will appear as nothing to him and disappear so that no sign of it remains because of his love for governing, which overwhelms it.

Therefore, the prophets, saints, and devout Muslims—even though they favor their wives, children, city, and country—when the love of God Most High appears and the pleasure of intimacy with Him appears, everything else becomes unimportant. This pleasure appears with death, so they are safe from (the torment of the grave). But there are those who love the carnal appetites of the world more (than God) and they shall not escape this torment; a majority are of this (group).

It is for this that God Most High said: *There is not one of you but shall approach it. That is the fixed ordinance of thy Lord. Then We shall rescue those who kept from evil, and leave the evil-doers crouching there.* (Q. 19:71-2) These people will suffer torment for a time. Then, as their commitment to the world grows distant, they forget the world and the pleasures of the world and see again the verity (*asl*) of the love of God Most High that has been in their hearts. They are like the person who prefers one mansion to another, or one city to another, or one wife to another, but he likes the others too. Separation will be painful for a while; then he forgets and becomes accustomed to the other. But his first affection is in his heart and returns even after a long time. However, the person who has absolutely no love of God Most High stays in that torment, for his love is for that which is taken back from him. By what consolation will he achieve liberation from that?

This is one of the reasons that the torment of the unbeliever is eternal.

Know that every one claims that he loves God Most High, or loves Him more than he loves the world, this is the practice of the whole world in word. But there are criteria and standards by which to recognize him (who speaks the truth). This is when his self and his appetite command him to do something, and the Law of God Most High commands something contrary to that. If one sees that his heart is more inclined to the command of God Most High, then he loves Him more; just as a person loves two friends, but loves one more than the other. If a dispute arises between his friends, he will take the side of the one whom he loves more and in this manner reveals which one he prefers. There are no ifs or buts. Uttering it with the tongue has no profit if the utterance is a lie.

It was with respect to this that the Prophet (ﷺ) said: "By always repeating 'there is no god but God' they are protected from the punishment of God, may He be honored and glorified, until they choose the bargain of the world over the bargain of religion. When they do that, God Most High calls them liars because their uttering of 'there is no god but God' was a lie."

So, from this you have learned that with internal witnessing the spiritually insightful see who will be delivered from the torment of the grave. They know that most people will be delivered, but they will be for a time in differing straits, according to the many different degrees of their ties to the world.

11 The Way to Test Safety From the Torment of the Grave

Again, there is a group of fools and presumptuous persons who say: "If this be the torment of the grave, we will be free of it, for we have no connections with the world; its existence or non-existence is nothing to us!" This claim is absurd; for until one tests it, one would not know. If it were thus, it would not have any effect upon his heart should whatever he has be stolen by a thief, every concession he has go to another—from among his companions—and all of his students turn away from him and slander him; it would be the same (to him) as though someone else's property were carried away or someone else's concession nullified. Then this claim would be just. It would be proper for him to say: "I have this character." But he is deluded so long as he is not robbed or they have not turned away from him. Therefore, he must separate himself from his wealth and pass up his rents and test himself; then he will have confidence. Many people have thought that they had no attachment to their wives and bondmaids, but when they divorce or sell them, the fire of love that was concealed in their hearts reappears and they become mad and miserable.

Consequently, anyone who desires to be delivered from the torment of the grave must not be attached to anything of this world, except by necessity. Just as every person has a need for a place of purification, he likes that out of necessity, yet wishes to be rid of it. His eagerness to put food in his stomach must be the same as in eliminating food from it; both are necessary. All other acts are like this.

Therefore, if the heart cannot be devoid of these attachments, one must make a fondness for the remembrance of God Most High dominant in one's heart by being attentive to worship and the remembrance of God Most High, so that this love masters the love of the world. One seeks proofs and evidence of this from oneself by following of the Religious Law and giving precedence to the command of God Most High over one's own passion. If the self obeys one (in these observances), one may be confident that he has escaped the torment of the grave. If this is not the case, he will lay his body upon the torment of the grave, unless God Most High's forgiveness touches him and helps him.

12 The Three Kinds of Spiritual Hellfire

Now it is the time for us to explain the meaning of "spiritual hell." By "spiritual," we mean that which pertains to the spirit exclusively: the body is excluded. *This is the fire of God, kindled, which leaps over the hearts (of men).* (Q. 104:6-7) It is the fire which overwhelms the heart, while that fire which attacks the body is called "physical."

So, know that there are three kinds of fire in spiritual hell: one is the fire of separation from the carnal appetites of the world; the second is the fire of shame, abashment, embarrassment, and disgrace; and the third is the fire of being deprived of the beauty of the Divine Presence and the loss of hope for that. All three of these fires affect the spirit and the heart, not the body. It is necessary to explain the causes of these three fires which they have carried with themselves from this place, and to make this meaning plain by borrowing comparisons from this world.

(i) The description of the first fire: This is being cut off from lust or carnal appetites of the world. The cause of this has been discussed (above) in the torment of the grave: The love of the necessary is the heaven of the heart and the hell of the animal soul. It is heaven as long as one is with the beloved and hell in the absence of the beloved. So the lover of the world is in heaven in this world: the world is the heaven of the unbelievers. But in the Hereafter he is in hell, because his beloved (the world) has been taken away from him. Consequently, one thing is both the cause of pleasure and also sorrow, but in two different circumstances.

The similitude of this fire in the world is a king who rules and is obeyed throughout the world and continually indulges himself in the enjoyment of beauties of girls and boys and wives, or in the admiration of beautiful gardens and palaces. Suddenly the enemy appears and captures him and carries him off in bondage. In his own country he is made a keeper of dogs! His family, concubines, and male captives are used before his very eyes! Everything in the treasury that was precious to him is given to his enemies. Think what sorrow this man will experience! The fire of separation from his power, women, children, bondmaids, blessings, and treasury will ignite in his mind and burn continuously. He would rather that they had killed him in some manner so that he could escape so much torment! This is the similitude of one fire. However much his ease was greater, his power more absolute and felicitous, the hotter the fire will burn.

Therefore, the love of him whose enjoyment in this world was greater and whom the world favored more will be more intractable and the fire of being cut off will burn more brightly in his spirit. Yet, it is not possible to find the likeness of the fire (of spiritual hell) in this world, for the sorrow of the animal soul that is in this world is not completely established in the heart and spirit. The senses and obligations of this world engage the heart, and those activities are like a curtain for the heart so that torment cannot become firmly established in it. The reason for this is that when the eyes and ears are occupied with something (else) a person's sorrow is diminished; but when they cease, it increases. It is for this reason that when a sorrowing person awakens from sleep, the pain of the misfortune on the heart is greater, for the spirit had been purified during sleep. Before perceptions return (upon awakening), whatever reaches him has a greater effect so that if one hears a sweet voice upon awakening, its effect is greater. The reason for this is the purification of the heart from sensory perceptions (during sleep). It is never completely purified in this world, but at death it becomes stripped and purified of sensory perceptions. At that time its sorrow and ease is stupendous and firmly fixed in his heart. Take care! Do not suppose that that fire will be like the fire of this world; rather, this fire (of this world) has been washed seventy times, then sent to the world.

(ii) The description of the second fire: That is the fire of shame and abashment from disgrace and humiliation. It will be like this: a king selects a base and tightfisted man and makes him his vizier in his kingdom. He gives him license to enter his women's quarters without their covering themselves before him. He entrusts his treasury to him and has confidence in him in all tasks. Then, when that man attains ease, he rebels and mutinies in his heart and misappropriates from the king's treasury. He betrays the king and corrupts the king's family and women. But outwardly, he shows himself to be trustworthy to the king. Then, one day while he is engaged in corruption in the women's quarters, he looks and sees the king looking through a small window and watching him. He knows that he has been observed every day and that the king was delaying until the vizier had made his betrayal even greater so that the king could make an example of him in some manner and kill him. In such a predicament imagine what a fire of embarrassment from this disgrace was burning in the heart and spirit of that man! And while his body was sound, in that condition he wishes that he could sink into the earth so as to escape the fire of shame, confusion, and infamy.

So, even as you perform tasks in this world, out of habit, which apparently seem good, yet their spirit and true nature are ugly and disgraceful. When the spirit and true nature of the thing are disclosed to you at the Resurrection and your disgrace revealed to all, you will be burned by the fire of abashment. For example, today you speak ill of some one, tomorrow at the Resurrection you will see that as though a person is eating the flesh of his brother and thinks he is eating roast chicken! When he looks, it is the flesh of his own brother that he is eating! See how it would be, how disgraced he will be! What fire will touch his heart! For this is the spirit and true nature of backbiting. This spirit of yours is rotten; that will be plainly evident tomorrow (at the Resurrection). It is for this that when a person dreams that he is eating carrion flesh, the interpretation is that he is backbiting.

If you throw a stone at a wall today and someone informs you that the stone has fallen from the wall into the house and put out the eye of one of your children, when you enter the house and see that the eye of one of your dear children has been blinded by that stone, do you know what fire will flame up in your heart and how ashamed you will become then? A person who in this world envies a Muslim will see himself in that shape at the Resurrection, for the true nature of his envy and his heart is that you aim to harm him with your enmity, but the harm is coming back to you and destroying your religion. Your acts of devotion, which would have been your delight in that world, are transferred to that person so that you are stripped of (the merit of that) devotion. Devotion will be more useful to you tomorrow than the eyes of your children today, which are the cause of your happiness. But children will not be the cause of your (spiritual) happiness. Therefore, tomorrow when forms become the followers of the spirits and true natures, everything they see will be seen as befits its spiritual significance. There will be disgrace and abashment there.

For the reason that sleep is closer to the other world, acts in sleep are in a form closer to (their) spiritual significance. As when a person went to Ibn Sirin and said: "In my sleep I saw that there was a ring in my hand and I was sealing the vulvas of women and the mouths of men." (Ibn Sirin) said: "You are a caller to formal prayer. In the month of Ramadan do you give the call to formal prayer before the dawn?" The other replied" That is so."

Now look how the spirit and true nature of his actions were shown to him in sleep. The call to formal prayer is in the form of a sound and a reminder that during Ramadan his spirit and true nature prevent eating and sexual intercourse (during the daylight hours). It is remarkable that all of these proofs of the Resurrection are shown to you during sleep, yet you yourself are not aware of their significance. It is related in the Traditions that on the Day of Resurrection the world will be brought up in the form of an ugly old hag, and so forth. Whoever sees her will say: "We seek refuge with God from thee!" It will be said (to them): "This is that world for which you destroyed yourself in seeking it!" They will be so ashamed—whoever sees her—that they will want to be taken off to hell in order to escape that ignominy.

The parable of this disgrace is this story which they tell: "One of the kings gave a woman to his son. On that night the king's son drank too much wine. When he was drunk he went out to find his wife. Heading for the bridal chamber, he became lost and went out of the palace. He continued walking until he reached a place where a lamp could be seen in a house. He thought that he found the bride's room. Upon entering, he saw some people sleeping. No matter how much he called out, no one answered him. He thought they were all asleep. He saw one person sleeping under a new wrapper. He said to himself: 'This must be my bride.'

"He lay down beside her and removed the wrapper from her. A sweet smell reached his nostrils. 'Doubtless this is my bride,' he said to himself, 'she is using such a fine scent.' He had intercourse with her until morning. He inserted his tongue into her mouth and he received some liquid from her. He thought that she was being very cordial and was pouring rose water on him.

"When day broke and he came to his senses, he looked about. It was a crypt of the fire worshippers! The sleepers were corpses! She who had the new wrapper, the one he thought was his bride, was an ugly old woman who had died nearby. The scent was her embalming spices, and the liquid that had flowed over was her filth! When he looked, he found himself completed covered with filth. There remained an acridity from her saliva in his mouth and throat. He was so mortified with shame and humiliation that he wished he could be struck dead. He feared that his father might come with his army and find him in this condition. And while he was pondering this, the king and commanders of his army came in search of him. They saw him in the middle of his shameful act. He wished that the earth would open up and swallow him so as to escape this ignominy."

So, tomorrow the people of the world and all its pleasures and carnal appetites will all appear thus. The traces that remain of the commerce of the carnal appetite in their animal souls will resemble her filth and the bitterness which remained in his throat and mouth and on his body, but will be even more shameful and horrendous.

The reality of the working of that world cannot be comprehended by parables from this world; however, this is an illustration of the description of one of the fires which burns in (one's) heart and spirit, while his body is unaware of it. It is the fire of shame and abashment.

(iii) The description of the third fire: (This is) the fire of regret. This is being deprived of the beauty of the Divine Presence and losing the hope of ever achieving that happiness. Its cause is the blindness and ignorance that (the heart), which has not acquired gnosis (*marifat*) by study or the greater struggle, takes with it from this world. Also, the heart has not been purified so that the beauty of the Divine Presence may be made manifest in it after death; there is no reflection in the mirror if the tarnish of sins and the appetites of the world have darkened one's heart to the extent that one remains blind.

The similitude of this fire is that you imagine that you are with some people. You arrived at a place in the dark of night where there are a lot of pebbles, but their colors cannot be seen. Your companions say: "Take as many of these pebbles as you can, because we have heard that there is great profit in them."

So every one of them picks up as many as he can, but you do not pick up anything. You say: "It is absolute foolishness for me to trouble myself and burden myself with a heavy load for the present when I don't even know whether they will be of any use tomorrow!"

Then the others leave that place carrying heavy loads, but you accompany them empty-handed and laughing at them, taking them for fools. You ridicule them and say: "Anyone who has reason and wisdom travels in ease and calmness, just as I am doing! Anyone who is a fool makes of himself an ass to carry a burden out of greed for the absurd!"

When day dawns and the sun's light shines, they look at their burdens. All of the pebbles are jewels and red rubies! The price of each stone is a hundred thousand dinars. Then the people were full of regret, saying: "Why did we not take more?" And you who have cheated yourself by not taking anything, you are mortified and the fire of regret flares in your spirit.

So they sell their jewels and with the money purchase power and ease in the land, eat what they desire, and live where they choose. But you! For you there is hunger and nakedness. You are enslaved and given hard tasks to perform. No matter how much you say to them: "Give me a portion of your ease,"—*'Pour on us some water or some of that wherewith God hath provided you.' They say: 'Lo! God hath forbidden both to the disbelievers, who took their religion for a sport and pastime*; (Q. 7:50-1)—they say: "Yesterday you were laughing at us; today we are laughing at you." *Though ye laugh at us, yet we laugh at you even as ye are laughing.* (Q. 11:38)

This is the parable of the regret at the loss of the blessings of heaven and seeing the Divine Presence, and the treasure is the metaphor of the acts of devotion. The darkness is the metaphor of the world. But those who did not pick up the jewels of devotion and said: "Now, why should we trouble ourselves in the present for a credit (to be charged to) comfort (in the future) about which there is a doubt?"—they will cry out tomorrow: '*Pour water on us . . .*' (Q. 7:50) Why should they not be regretful? For tomorrow God will shower so many different kinds of happiness and comfort upon the gnostics (knowers, mystics) and the devout that the comforts of this world could not compete with them for an instant! On the contrary, the least person who is introduced into hell is given ten times (the torment) of this world. This similitude is not of dimension and amount; rather, it is in the spirit of comfort, and that is joy and pleasure. As they say: A jewel is like ten dinars in value and spirit, not in opulence, weight, and dimension.

13 Spiritual Fire Is More Terrible Than Physical Fire

You have become acquainted with the three kinds of spiritual fire. Now, know that this fire is more terrible than that which consumes the body, for the body is not aware of pain so long as its effect does not reach the vital spirit; then, the pain from the body reaches the vital spirit and becomes terrible. Consequently, the fire and pain which comes out of the vital spirit, is certainly greater. This fire ignites from within the vital spirit and does not come in from outside.

The cause of all kinds of pain is that a thing required by nature becomes contrary to it and takes possession over it. It is required by the nature of the body that it maintain its structure and that its parts be agreeable together. Should an injury separate them, one from another, its contrary appears; it becomes painful. The wound separates one part from another, but a fire burns in all parts and separates the (all the) parts from one another. Then each part receives the pain from another. For this reason, the pain of the fire is greater.

So, the pain of that thing which is required by the nature of the heart, should its contrary become established, is greater within the vital spirit. The requirement of the nature of the heart is the gnosis of God and seeing Him. Should blindness, which is contrary (to the requirement of the nature of the heart), become established in it, there is no end to its pain. If it were not the case that hearts become sick in this world before death, the pain of blindness (to the gnosis of God) would be perceived in this world in like manner. But just as hands and feet become exhausted and numbness appear in them so that if fire touched them, one would not know it immediately. If the numbness passes and (the member) is in the fire, one instantly feels great pain. In the same way, hearts become fatigued in this world (and do not feel the fire), but that numbness departs at death. The fire flares in one's vital spirit instantly. This does not come from some other place, for he has brought it himself with himself. It was inside his heart, but since he did not have firm belief, he had not spotted it until he knew with sure vision. *Nay, would that ye knew with a certain knowledge! For ye will behold hell-fire*. (Q. 102:5-6)

The reason that the Religious Law has explained and described physical hell and heaven so much is so that all people may know and understand it. However, whatever you say, these words are considered modest, for they do not convey the harshness (of hell) and magnitude (of heaven). It is as though you say to a child: "Learn something, for if you do not, your father's power and authority will not be left to you and you will never achieve happiness." (The child) will not comprehend this and it will not seem very important to him. However, if you say: "The teacher will punish you," he will be afraid of this, because he understands it. Just as the teacher's punishment is real, but the fire of being deprived of the rank of his father, though also real, will not chastise a child, so too, the physical hell is real as is the fire of being deprived of the beauty of the Divine Presence. The physical hell in comparison with the hell of deprivation is nothing more than a box on the ears when put beside the deprivation of power and authority.

14 The Stations of the Travels of the Spirit in the World

Certainly you may object that this explanation and detailed account is contrary to that which all of the religious scholars say and that which is found in books. They have said that these matters cannot be known save by following authority and listening. There is no room for the insight in this.

Know that the nature of their objection to this is has already been noted. This discourse is not contrary to that; for everything that they have said in the exposition of the Hereafter is correct. However, it does not go beyond an exposition of the perceptible things. Either they did not know about the spiritual aspects, or they knew, but did not expound upon them, because most people would not comprehend them.

Anything which is physical will not be made known except by following the authority of and listening to a scholar of the Religious Law. However, the other part is a branch of the gnosis of the true nature of the spirit. There is a way to learn this by means of insight and internal witnessing. It comes to the person who has separated himself from his own homeland and not stayed where he was born and in his home. He embarks on the journey on the path of religion. By this homeland we do not mean a city or house which is the homeland of the body; the journey of the body has no value. Instead, (we mean the homeland of) the spirit which is the true nature and inmost mystery of a human being. It has a resting place which has appeared from there and its homeland is there; hence it has to make a journey. Along the road there are stages for (the heart), and each station is another world.

Its first station is perceptible things, then imaginings, then suppositions, and then probabilities, which is the fourth station. It is in this fourth station that one will find the true nature of one's self. Before that it has no knowledge of it.

(1) The first station: These worlds may be understood by a parable: as long as a person is in the world perceptible things, his degree is similar to that of a moth which throws itself against a lamp. It has the sense of sight, but not thought and memory. It flies from the darkness seeking an opening. It thinks that the lamp is a window and throws itself against it. When it feels the pain of the fire, that pain does not stay in its memory, nor in its thought, because it has no thought or memory as it has not achieved that degree. Consequently, it dashes itself against the lamp again and again until it perishes. If it had had the faculties of thought and the memory of imaginings, it would not have returned after one painful experience. When other (higher) animals are struck once, they will run away whenever they see a stick, for its image has remained in their memories. Therefore, the first stage is of perceptions.

(2) The second station: imaginings. As long a person is at this degree, he is the equal of the beasts. Until he experiences some irritation, he does not know that he should flee. However, if he is discomfited once, he knows to flee the next time.

(3) The third station: suppositions. When one reaches this degree, he is at the level of sheep and horses, which flee from unseen trouble, for they know it is an enemy and may injure them. A sheep may never have seen a wolf, and a horse may never have seen a lion, but when a wolf or lion is spotted, they

flee and know that it is an enemy, while they do not run away from cattle, elephants, or camels which are much larger in size. This is a discernment which has been implanted in them by means of which they recognize their own enemies. But with all of this, they are not able to take precautions against that which may happen tomorrow, which is in:

(4) The fourth station: This is the station of probabilities. When a person arrives here he has passed the limit of all animals. Up to this point he has been accompanying them. In fact, it is here that he truly reaches the world of humanity. He sees things to which the senses, images, and suppositions cannot go, and which caution him about the future. He wrests the spirit and true nature of matters from their appearance and perceives them (as they truly are). He perceives the limit of the true nature of everything, (the true nature of) which comprises the totality of that thing's forms. The things which can be perceived in this world are not infinite, for everything which is perceptible by the senses does not exist except in physical bodies, and physical bodies cannot be other than finite.

One's traffic and walking in the world of perceptible things is like walking on the earth, which all people can do. One's walking in the fourth world—in purely spirits and the true natures of affairs—is like walking on water. One's traffic in suppositions is like being in a ship, and one's degree is between water and land.

There is a station beyond the level of probabilities which is the station of the prophets, saints, and spiritually insightful: its similitude is like traveling on air. It was for this that the Prophet (ﷺ) was asked: "Did Jesus (عليه السلام) walk on water?" He answered: "That is true, but if his certainty had been greater, he would have traveled through the air."

Therefore, the stages of a person's journey are in the worlds of perceptions until one reaches the last of the stations, which is at the degree of the angels. So, the stations of the human ascension are from the last degree of the beasts to the highest degrees of the angels, and the ups and downs of this enterprise. One is in danger of falling to the lowest depths instead of reaching the highest heights. With reference to this danger, (this verse) was revealed: *Surely We offered the trust to the heavens and the earth and the mountains, but they shrank from bearing it and feared it; and man bore it. Surely, he is unjust, ignorant.* (Q. 33:72)

Look at the degree of every inanimate solid body. It is unaware, therefore it is without rank. The angels are in the highest; for them there is no way beyond their own level. Indeed, the degree of every one is established upon him, as is said: *And there is none of us but has an assigned place.* (Q. 37:164) The (four-legged) beasts are the lowest of the low; there is no way for them to advance. Mankind is between the two and in a dangerous place. It is possible for him to ascend to the level of the angels or to descend to the level of the beasts. The meaning of "bearing of trust" is "assuming the covenant of danger." Consequently, it is not possible for other than a human being to carry the burden of this trust.

The point is that if you said: "Most people have not said this," you would know that it is not unusual for a traveler to be contrary to settled people. Most people are residents; the traveler is the exception. A person who has made sensory perceptions and images—the first station—his home and residence, will never uncover the truths and spirits of affairs. He will not be spiritual, nor will he know the rules of the spiritual. It is for that reason that there is less discussion about this in books.

15 Denial of the Hereafter Based Upon Weak Suppositions Is Also Unlawful

There is a party of fools who do not possess the power to

know such matters insightfully, nor do they possess the good fortune to accept Religious Law. They are perplexed by the matter of the Hereafter and have become overcome by doubt. It may be that, as carnal appetite begins to overwhelm them and—as befits their nature—inspires them to deny the Hereafter, this denial is born in them. Satan teaches this. They think that all that has come (to us) about the nature of hell is to inspire fear, and that all that has been said about heaven is blandishment. For these reasons, they indulge in following their appetite and cease to apply the Religious Law (to themselves). They despise those who do follow the Religious Law, saying: "They have cheated themselves and are deceived."

Where is there the power to inform such a fool about such secrets and proofs? Consequently, he must be invited to reflect upon one plain saying. He is told: "Even though your mind has been mastered by the idea that the 124,000 prophets, all the saints, religious scholars, and wise men were in error and were deluded, and that you in your own foolishness have discovered this situation; well, is it not possible that the error is yours, that you are the deluded one, that you have not learned the true nature of the Hereafter and have not understood spiritual chastisement, and that you have not learned the aspects and similitudes of spiritual matters from the world of perceptible things?"

If the case is that he does not allow his own error, but says: "As I know that two is greater than one, in the same way I know that the spirit itself has no reality and it is not eternal. There can be neither ease nor torment for it after death; neither spiritual, nor physical." This person has a ruined temperament, and one should not be optimistic about him. He is one of those people about whom God Most High said: *And if thou call them to the guidance, they will even then never follow the right course.* (Q. 18:57)

But if he says: "The impossibility of this does not matter

to me; that is, it is possible, but remotely. And since I do not consider this condition to be true, why should I spend my life in the cell of piety and be deprived of pleasures because of a weak supposition?"

Say to him: "Now that you have admitted this much, you are obligated by the rule of reason to follow the way of the Law; for, even if the suspicion of a great danger is weak, people will flee from it. If you intend to eat some food and some one says: 'A snake has bitten into that food!' you will withhold your hand from it, even though you suspect that that person may be lying and had said that so that he could eat it himself. However, since it is possible that he is speaking the truth, you say to yourself: 'If I do not eat it, I can bear the hunger easily, but suppose I eat it and he is telling the truth? I might die!'

"In the same way, if you fall ill and (your life) is in danger, and a charmer says to you: 'Give me a silver coin and I shall write a charm for you on paper and draw a design on it that will make you better.' However strong your belief is that an amulet has absolutely no connection with health, you say: 'Perhaps he is speaking the truth. Giving up a silver coin for the recitation is easy.' If an astrologer says to you: 'When the moon reaches such-and-such point, take such-and-such bitter medicine to become better.' You submit to that discomfort upon his word. You say: 'It may be that he is speaking the truth. If he is lying, still, enduring that difficulty is easy.'"

So, to a reasonable person, the word of 124,000 prophets, together with all of the great of the world, such as saints and wise men, is not less than the word of an astrologer or a charmer or a Christian physician so that, as (the sick person) says, he undertakes a small discomfort in order to escape a far greater sorrow and loss: it may be that he will obtain deliverance (from the illness). The sorrow and loss become trivial and relative. If a person calculates how long his life in this world is, and what a small fraction it is of the endless eternity which has no beginning with respect to the beginning—less eternity which has no end, he knows that taking a little trouble is insignificant when set beside such great peril. He says to himself: "If they are speaking the truth, and I endure in such torment, what is the profit of the ease of this world, the days of which are passing few? And it is possible that they speak the truth?"

Eternity means that if the entire world were filled with millet and a bird was ordered to pick up one grain of millet every thousand years until all of that millet was consumed, eternity would not be at all diminished. Therefore, how can one endure that much time in torment—whether it be spiritual, physical, or mental? How great is the span of a life in this world in comparison with that? There is no reasonable person who, understanding this concept fully, does not know that proceeding along the path of caution and being wary of such a great danger is imperative, even though this causes some trouble and even though one has this suspicion. People travel in ships across the sea for trade. They undertake long journeys and endure many hardships. They all do this for an uncertain supposition. If (the Hereafter) is not certain for a man, well, there is a weak supposition. So, if one has mercy on oneself, one considers (the Hereafter) a possibility.

It was concerning this that the Commander of the Believers, Ali, may God be pleased with him, debated an atheist and said: "If it is as you say, both you and we are delivered. But if it is as we say, we are delivered and you are fallen and will remain in eternal torment."

This which the Commander of the Believers, Ali, may God be pleased with him, said, he said in accordance with the deficiency of the intelligence of that atheist, not because he himself had any doubts about his faith. He knew that that atheist's understanding could not support the way of certainty.

So, know that whoever busies himself with anything other

that providing for the Hereafter is extremely foolish. The reason for this is heedlessness and not thinking. The carnal appetites of the world themselves will not give them respite long enough to think about these things. If that were not so, it would be obligatory upon that person who knows with certainty, that person who knows with a strong supposition, and that person who knows with a weak supposition—-all of them, by the rule of reason—to be wary of that great danger and take up the way of safety and caution. Peace! . . . .